Smith's Expressions

Written By : Christopher C. Smith

Christopher C. Smith
Father, Author, Actor, Independent Publisher & Song Writer

Durrell Mohammad better known by his stage name **Hell Rell**, is an American rap artist and member of rap group The Diplomats. Rell started his own label.Topgunnas in 2008. Since 2008 Hell Rell has drop 5 independent albums follow from the deal he had with Koch Records working on his debut album, *For the Hell Of It* The album reached #5 on both the *Billboard* Top Independent Albums and Top Rap Albums chart, and #10 on the Top R&B/Hip-Hop Album also 12 solo mixtapes. Topgunnas is also a group with a few artist such as G-five, TouchMoney R/A ,

No More State Greens
The Autobiography Urban Novel
out now !!!!

EYE SII PHOTOGRAPHY

George Perkins, owner and photographer of Eye Sii Photography. Nestled in the suburbs of Chicago, Eye Sii Photography started with a simple camera phone and a dream. This company has now evolved to being one of the well known photography companies throughout Chicago with picture perfection in Weddings to Portrait and Head-shots for the cast of NBC's hit series Chicago PD. To contact us email us at eyesiiphotography@gmail.com

"The Original Hip Hop Shop"

With much gratitude and many thanks to 1st Born (President of Iron Fist Global), Benjamin Brothers and Associates, and many others "The Original Hip Hop Shop" is back again for the first time! Although located in the exact location as Maurice Malone's Hip Hop Shop, which closed in 1998, The Original Hip Hop Shop is NOT affiliated with Malone. The grand opening started of with a 21 Mic Salute honoring DeShaun Dupree Holton aka Big Proof on October 2nd 2014 which also happens to be Proofs birthday. We are committed to preserving the Culture while dedicating honors to the memory of Iconic Legends of Hip Hop creating "Opportunities within its Community" for aspiring artists to pursue their entrepreneurial dreams

Thanks & Dedication's

First I would like to give thanks to God

My Beautiful Mother
Ora Henderson

My Beautiful daughter
Lauren Smith

G – five & Hell Rell
My Top Gunnas family
Trippy Casino & Julio Monreal
Neme Cancel & the PBF Fam
Shacora Johnson
Erik Felix & Fayiz Abidi
Joahua Quesada
Moe Dirdee
Amy & Nikki From Detroit
Jave & KonCept from L.A.
Christopher Bullock
Darrell Washington
Cash Blocka & the whole B.G.G
D'Juan Garcia & Aaron Thomas
Ophelia Smith & MarQuetta Davis
Mrs Carrie
Bonnie & James
and everyone at #5404
And anyone else I forgot, I thank you

"Music & Me"

Started in the 90's
listening to Big and Pac
moved on to Master p
Jay z with the Roc
back when Ja had it popping
Diddy couldn't be stopped
he had Mase, Faith and Rob
but had just lost the Lox
so I picked a pen and pad
started jotting down my dreams
never thought within these years
that this is what I'd be
I done lost a few friends
made lots of enemies
thinking they was really down
how stupid silly me
then I started up a team at the age of 17
now I rock my own clothes
logo's stitched in the jeans
then I started traveling
and I hit the Philly scene
met a few celebs there
then I hit the Cali streets
drove around most places
most cats couldn't see
from the things that I've accomplished
hope that you are proud of me
so im back home now
tellin yall of what I seen,
if you don't believe me
feel free to google me

"Change"

I'm a make a change
And that's changing myself,
I don't know if I'm a make it
So I pray for my self
Looking for success, not days in a cell
playing cards I was dealt
to the fame and the wealth
Give a fuck bout a hater
Because I made it my self
Think I'm dead wrong
then you playing your self
It was days I had struggled
was like living in hell
with the faith in the lord
I refuse to jus fail
Now I'm walking down a road
I had paved for my self
Grinding with the clothes
and the music as well
so if you ever feeling down
hope my music can help
because next thing you know
I'm making moves by myself
what them others dudes did
I can do by myself
but prolly even better
at not losing my self
or have to move a finger
may be loosin my belt
so when it's said and done
I made a change for the best

"Letter From Your Youngest"

When others look down at your youngest
You still smiled
Because it was something deep down
That you found in your youngest
So I'm never giving up
Till your proud of your youngest
From sticking by my side
And walking miles with your youngest
You kept me a float
When life was drowning your youngest
When I was down and out
You kept a smile on your youngest
You played both parents
When Pops wasn't round for your youngest
So I thank God
For blessing me with a Mom
Like your youngest !!!!!!

LOVE YOU MOM

"History the Remix"

Slavery stills exists
But when we seek they try to hide it
So we got to stick together
Stand strong and try to fight it
Hoping God will stand beside us
Give us strength
and help us fight it
Because knowing they don't like us
They be quick to try and indict us
So we form our groups
start storming through
The places they don't let us
So peep the game we bleed the same
You all are pretty much just like us
So the hate should die
don't try to take our lives
But help our guys
that need it
Because you'll be surprised
that most my kind our pretty much a genius.

"My Ambitions"

For those that steady hated
Only motivate me more
To continue with the grind
To they just start to hate me more
From the struggling in fact
To the travels across the maps
I done came along way
Never thought of turning back
Just to see how far I come
Can't forget about where I'm from
I never gave up on my dreams
All that hate built self esteem
Because knowing life changes
In the blink of an eye
I don't know where I'm going
So my heads to the sky
If I fell oh well just as long as I tried
To stand tall on my feet and continue to grind
Saying smith ain't making moves
Then you speaking a lie
I done been through hell and back
yet still I survive
I was told I'd hit the top
in matter of time
so if u thought I was over
take a look at me now
steady proving haters wrong
don't have the urge to speak now
got the speakers banging loud ain't no turning me down

"It's over"

Feeling's shared
Years invested
Who would've thought I'd soon regret it
Broken hearts
Deep depressions
Plans of marriage some how vanished
The time we spent was truly blessings
Things we planned could only imagine
The life I chose
That made this happen
From reaching my goals
To getting established
Accomplishing both was hard to manage
Female fans didn't quite understand it
Now I'm alone and can't really stand it
Looking at the pics we took from cameras
Trying my best
But it's hard to stand when
Seeing you in the arms of another man when
What we shared is some how damaged
& it's because of my dreams
That this had happened

"Fresh Start"

Failed plenty times
But won't let it get the best of me
Learning from mistakes
And what I thought was really best for me
Hanging out with friends
Who I thought would want the best for me
True colors showed
But surprised how they envied me
Thinking they was down
How stupid really silly me
Lost sight of goals
And everything that was important to me
Now I'm back on track
And refuse to go that route again
Been through hell and back
With more reasons jus to smile again
Whatever don't kill me
Only make me strong again
Haters once laughed
Now I see they start to frown again
Instead they give me props
At one time they was downing him
Building up my buzz
And I did it on my own again
Praying on my down fall
While looking down on him
Lost plenty friends
Now I see they come around again
Soza be home soon
Can't wait till he home again
My Mother's youngest child
So I'm making sure she proud of him.

"Brand New Me"

I'm through selling dreams
And the stupid lies you bought
Things ain't been the same
So who am I to talk
To put aside the drama
unless you and I can talk
So let me state that I was wrong
From the stupid times we fought
Left you in this cold world
To face it on your own
Must've been a strong girl
To see you made it on your own
So I'm asking for this marriage
I can't make it on my own
Because that house we once shared
I'm here to make into a home.

"My Love Lives On"

Barely met my pops
Still became a better guy
Never really held a grudge
I just put my pride a side
So in case I die tonight
No, I never lost your love
Even though you wasn't there 4 me
When I was growing up
So I'm wishing you the best
Hoping you'll meet success
Though we finally met
It never once caused me stressed
I thank God for my Mom
Because of that I've been blessed
& with my daughter by my side
Best believe she'll be set !!!!

"Life Guard"

You came at a time
When my heart was wounded
And bandaged up my scars and bruises
Late night talks
When I thought I'd lose it
To being there for me
To walk me through it
Really helped a lot
As serious as it got
Never would've thought
I'd be as far as what I got
With you by my side
Love will never die
So I put a side my pride
When others would've lied
So I,
I was looking back at the road I took
and how shit seems
in the start of the midst
I was ready to quit
& damn near give up on my dreams
but until you came along
& really got involved
it was like
You was sent from the man up above
Because you came just in time
right before I drowned
if I didn't know it then
shit I bet I know it now

"She is There"

Time has passed and things has changed
Days go by and seasons changed
I thank you now for things you changed
You shield the rain and cure my pain
But if u left wouldn't be the same
Because when we met
I knew that day
My life had changed
In major ways I'm proud to say
By sitting back
By seeing us both
I'm feeling blessed to be us both
I pray to god he keep us close
Never thought he involved us both
Planting seeds to them grow
I'm grinding hard to feed us both
Dodging hell has brought us close
So I cherish moments as we grow

"Friend's Expressions"
(Poems)

"Words"
Written by: Myth
(of Point Blank Fam Inc.)

Words of love ,words of hate Words
destroy, but words create words bring
conflict, words start situations Words create
love, words create complications words
create bonds, words create hope Words are
the language ,of our inner soul With out
words, there is no passion   So at the end,
words are just words with no actions words
motivate, words express love words bring
hate and words break trust words are the
gateways, to ones lust Words bring joy
while some words devour us words express
our reasons, words solve our problems
words start wars but words written with the
pen, mightier than the swords Words bring
you to dark places, but words create beauty
And when words break you down, its
someone's words who are soothing See
words are powerful to those who abuse it
But with out actions, sometimes words are
useless

"Loyalty First Respect After"
Written by Neme Cancel
(Of Point Blank Fam Inc.)

Loyalty First Respect After, seems like that story changes with every chapter..
You can't please everyone but yet that's something we all try to master, and now what was once picture perfect is now a disaster..
What's a friend? Someone who is there until the end..who takes u as u are and no need to pretend.. because nowadays that fades away like the ink from a pen..
Friend or Enemy ? Got u thinking again..
Respect is not often earned but is expected to be given..
It's like a joke nowadays but who are all of us kidding..
We give more respect to the dead than we do the living..
Playing devil's advocate but we're suppose to all be gods children..
secrets and lies is something we each try to hide..
Because the truth may hurt too much so we tend to keep it inside..
Some may reach for the sky but end up underground/..
Because Loyalty is lost once the Respect is not found..
Like karma what goes around comes around so you're better off being solo..
Cuz loyalty and respect can easily disappear like deleting a photo..

"Lost In Thought"
Written By Sweeny
(Of Point Blank Fam Inc)

My nomadic heart ignited by poetic sparks
And with a simple thought I illuminate the dark
Some people won't believe the truth and it don't matter
how you put it
Who we fooling man the truth is we want to believe the
bullshit
Ignorance is bliss but the knowledge is the power
Where only the strong survive your ignorance gets you
devoured
I pour out my heart with every word it's like a shower
You won't say it how you feel that's how I know you're
just a coward
Look how time flies damn how the days pass
A second so precious a moment is too fast
I'm trying to make it last but it's draining all of my energy
I swear the hardest thing I'll do is trying to leave a
memory
Sometimes I can't stand the pressure and I clam up
Trying to get my foot inside the door before it slams
shut
Trying to put my hands on something I can't touch
To the point I would give me life never wanted
something so much
But till the end I'll pursue with my last breath
I'm not at the place I'm a be at yet
Sometimes I write all night I just put my heart into it
Jus to see their faces when I'm into it
Yea I'm going to get it I feel it in my spirit
So u can feel it in my words even if u didn't hear it

"Reflections"
Written by Itzel
(Of Point Blank Fam Inc.)

All this memories and thoughts keep circling the head,

all the memories from the past keep running through the mind

like if it was a street racing competition.

Thinking of all the mistakes that occurred and all the lessons that were taught,

recognizing what all of that has given and the person that it has become.

Decisions are being made every second some good,

some bad with a lot of obstacles in front and with a lot of fear that only strength can go through with no doubt.

Fearing of the future and what is ahead,

thinking if the same mistakes would ever be made again.

Not knowing if the lessons are still clear or if they have vanished just like the tears that were shed once.

"Life and Music" _\|/_
Written by Trippy Casino
(Of Smg/HNEnt)

Music is my life
My life is the music
We choose to make it sound sweet because
our children use it!
Expressions and affiliation can determine a song.
Why Send a bad message?
Who hear and follow
To kill each other,
Our sons !!!
Music in life
has more potential
Then just hearing a song,
Wise minds is speaking pay attention u might
shine like the sun.
My message here is, if you realize our lives
music do move it
& while making music out of our lives
it can help us improve it
I proved it.,
Obstacles and problems out my way
I moved it ,
in front of me
Jesus leading my ways no way I blew it.!

#SMG #Casino

NO More State Greens

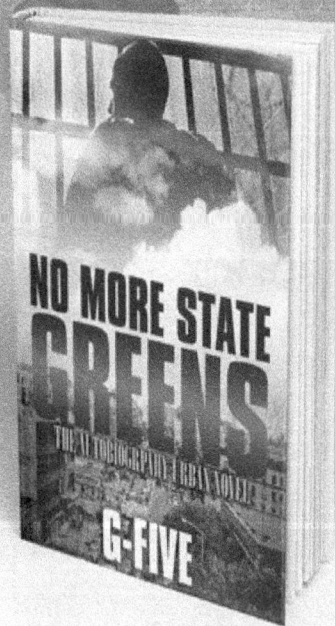

HUSTLE. SACRIFICE. SUCCESS.

G-FIVE
NO MORE STATE
GREENS
THE AUTOBIOGRAPHY URBAN NOVEL

NO MORE STATE
GREENS
THE AUTOBIOGRAPHY URBAN NOVEL
G-FIVE

#NOMORESTATEGREENS

Topgunna Promotions LLC
Published by Troy Hough
Written by Troy (G-Five) Hough
Contact: Nomorestategreen@gmail.com
Website: www.NoMoreStateGreen.com
InstaGram: @gfive_nomorestategreens
Facebook: Fivey Nomorestategreens
Cover Design by Keon Peterson @680 Media Group
Cover Design Contact: sixtyeightymedia@gmail.com
Instagram: @6080media

Note:
Sale of this book without an official front cover may be unauthorized. If this book was purchased without a cover or a duplicate cover, it may have been reported to the publisher as 'bootlegged' neither the author nor publisher may have received payment for the sale of this book.

ISBN: 978-0-692-25806-4

For All Store Orders Please visit our website www.nomorestategreens.com or contact Via Email NoMoreStateGreens@gmail.com

Printed in the United States

CHAPTER I

AUGUST 28, 1995 8:49PM

As the A Train pulls inside the station I eagerly waited for the doors to open up on 42nd street. As soon as both doors ajar I rushed off the cart in full speed bumping into passengers getting on & off the train. At the time I really didn't care, I had a bus to catch and getting to the Port Authority was the only thing on my mind. I still had about 11 minutes left before my bus departed at 9:00pm. At the age of 19 I was living life on the edge. I was already running the streets heavy, partying, playing with guns & selling drugs. I also had a big responsibility to take on and that was being a father to an 8 pound 6 ounces baby boy who was at the time 7 months old. That was the turning point in my life I had to step it up in the game & New York City wasn't cutting it so I took my hustle to another state.

I started out traveling back & forth out of town transporting drugs. I had big plans for the State of

Connecticut & getting rich was one of them. With no luggage, just the cloths I had on my back & a pocket full of drugs I was on my way. As I race through the Port Authority running behind schedule I still needed to purchase my bus ticket, but with 7 minutes left and 3 customers on line ahead of me there was no way in hell I was making that 9:00pm bus to New Britain C.T. As I approached the ticket counter the clock on the wall read 9:03pm. Behind the ticket counter stood a short Hispanic female about 5"4 with long jet black hair. I admit she was gorgeous, but her attitude was fucked up and nasty. By the looks of it she was having a bad day, but I didn't care so was I. I politely asked her was it

NoMoreStateGreens

Any way possible for her to find out if the 9:00pm Greyhound to New Britain C.T departed yet, if not was it even possible for her to have them hold for at least 5 more minute's. Without even taking her eyes off the computer screen her direct words to me was no she can't, that's not part of her job description. Normally I would have had something smart to say but with a pocket full of drugs I didn't want to draw any unnecessary attention to myself so I politely said thank you & for her to have a nice day. As I turn to walk away from the ticket counter the mood of her attitude must have change in a split of a second, because just 1 minute ago this same lady was acting like she didn't want to be bothered now was willing to help me out. She let me know that it was a 9:30pm Bonanza going to Boston that stops in Hartford Connecticut arrival time 12:30am will I be willing to catch that bus.

Being that New Britain is only 20 minutes away from Hartford I jumped right on it. The only difference was the price on the ticket, which was only $10.00 extra. After I paid for my ticket she let me know what gate my bus was departing from and I had about 15 minutes before it departed. Since I had 15 minutes to spare I made a quick stop at a concession stand located inside the Port Authority. I wasn't really hungry, so I just grab a Tropicana orange juice, 2 bags of Doritos potatoes chips and one of those Source Hip Hop magazines. When you are transporting drugs their is no special way to go about it either you going to get caught or you not, simple as that. Most people use mules to carry their drugs, females especially. For some reason people think females is the least, too be suspected, which is true some of the time but not all the time.

Females tend to get nervous under pressure especially if it, have anything with them going to jail. The first thing police say to

NoMoreStateGreens

Them, is that they going to take away their kids if they don't cooperate. That's their breaking point.

Now you do have a few that will hold it down, those are what we call that ride or die chick. It can be your girlfriend, that side chick, or even that neighborhood hood rat that's just down for whatever for a couple of dollars. Me personally I would never put a love one especially my girlfriend in that type of situation to transport any type of drugs for me, now that hood rat that's a different story. The only problem with them hood rat chicks is that they're never around when you really need them. Like this one chick from the hood name Keisha (aka) key-key she's down for whatever as long as you talking dollar signs. She's that one chick every drug dealer in the hood goes to when they need a crib to cook or bag up their drugs in. See Key-Key was a perfect example of a crack baby born in the 80's. Both of her parents was crack heads, her mother died giving birth to her little brother when she was 2 years old which left her to be raise by her grandmother. Her so called father never looked at her twice. By the time Key-Key turn 13 years old she was so out of control her grandmother had giving up on her. She was too much to handle, rumor was that Key-Key started turning tricks & fucking niggas for cash. Ever since she was young, Key-Key always found a way to make some money.

But today like I said she's know where to be found. They always say if you want something done the right way you have to do it yourself. So here am walking through the Port Authority with a pocket full of drugs and before I even get to the gate I'm approached by 3 Port Authority Police getting off the escalator. I'm not going to even front I was nervous ass hell and that weed I smoked 2 hours prior didn't make it no better. That African Black I copped from 124th

NoMoreStateGreens

& Madison had my eyes blood shot red.

At the time I was 19 years old but I had a face of a 16 years old kid. I had no facial hair on my face at all. They must have thought I was some type of runaway wondering around the Port Authority because the first question they ask me was where was my parents. I gave them the type of look like (what the fuck is you talking about) I'm 19 years old my mother is home. They must have thought I was lying about my age because as soon as I told them my age they ask me for some identification. At the time all I had on me was my old ass High School I.D, which had my date of birth on it, which had expired 2 years ago.

After showing them I was old enough, they wanted to know where was I headed which I stated to them back home to Connecticut. They wanted to know what was I doing in NYC if I lived in C.T? I answered every fucking question they ask but they could tell I was a little bit nervous which I was. The only thing on my mind was to take off running but I thought maybe I could talk my way out of it. They must have sense I was about to take off on them so they surrounded me just in case I made any moves. I definitely wasn't about to catch an assault on police so I just stood my grounds and didn't run. I didn't know it at the time but the police needed probable cause to even search me, which they didn't have. They took it upon themselves to start going through my pockets where they found me carrying a large amount of crack cocaine. I was placed under arrest and charged with possession of a control substance with the intent to sell 220.16.

www.ingramcontent.com/pod-product-compliance
Lightning Source LLC
Chambersburg PA
CBHW020954030426
42339CB00004B/94